PRAYER JOURNAL

THE
POWER
OF A
Praying®
Wife

Reflections from
STORMIE OMARTIAN

HARVEST HOUSE PUBLISHERS
Eugene, Oregon 97402

Cover by Koechel Peterson & Associates, Minneapolis, Minnesota

THE POWER OF A PRAYING® WIFE PRAYER JOURNAL
Copyright © 2002 by Stormie Omartian
Published by Harvest House Publishers
Eugene, Oregon 97402

ISBN 0-7369-0916-8

Printed in the United States of America

02 03 04 05 06 07 / DC-MS / 10 9 8 7 6 5 4 3 2 1

Welcome
to a life of prayer...

Keeping a prayer journal as you pray for your husband is probably one of the most important things you can do to benefit your marriage. Writing out your thoughts, feelings, desires, and conversations with God is not only healing and liberating, but it also gives you a fresh perspective on how to pray. I have found that as I put down my own thoughts and concerns on paper, I gain new insight into the very thing I am writing about. It gives me increased clarity. I find a deeper level of understanding about my husband, myself, our marriage, and the details of our lives together. You, too, can experience all that. But don't think of this as merely writing down a list of concerns. Think of it as sharing your heart with the Lord and expressing your deepest feelings and needs to Him. Think of it as presenting your thoughts, questions, and prayer requests to God and allowing Him to lift any burden from you and clear your mind of all worry and concern.

I pray that each of the short prayers and scriptures I have included here will inspire and motivate you to write in greater detail on those particular subjects, and to include any other areas of prayer need that they may bring to your mind. As you write, be sure to include anything God reveals to you or impresses upon your heart. He will speak to your soul through His Word or as you are in prayer. His words to you are as important as yours are to Him. Preserve them on these pages as precious gems. May God bless you and your marriage as you travel on this prayer journey with the Lord.

—STORMIE OMARTIAN

Continue earnestly in prayer, being vigilant in it with thanksgiving.

—COLOSSIANS 4:2

Lord, give me a fresh perspective, a positive outlook, and a renewed relationship with the man You've given me. Only You are perfect, and I look to You to perfect us. Help me see him with new eyes, new appreciation, new love, new compassion, and new acceptance. Teach me how to pray for my husband and make my prayers a true language of love. Make me a new person. Give my husband a new wife, Lord, and let it be me.

Prayer Journal

Prayer Journal

...teach me how to pray

But the fruit of the Spirit is love, joy, peace, longsuffering, kindness, goodness, faithfulness, gentleness, self-control.

—GALATIANS 5:22-23

Lord, make me my husband's helpmate, companion, champion, friend, and support. Help me to create a peaceful, restful, safe place for him to come home to. Teach me how to take care of myself and stay attractive to him. Grow me into a creative and confident woman who is rich in mind, soul, and spirit. Make me the kind of woman he can be proud to say is his wife.

Prayer Journal

Prayer Journal

_...helpmate, companion,
champion, friend_

When you eat the labor of your hands, you
shall be happy, and it shall be well with you.

—PSALM 128:2

Lord, I pray that my husband's work
will be established, secure, successful,
satisfying, and financially rewarding. I
pray that You will be Lord over his
work, and may he bring You into every
aspect of it. Give him enough confidence
in the gifts You've placed in him to be
able to seek, find, and do good work.
Open up doors of opportunity for him
that no man can close. Develop his skills
so that they grow more valuable with
each passing year. Show me what I can
do to encourage him.

Prayer Journal

Prayer Journal

...be Lord over his work

As for every man to whom God has given riches and wealth, and given him power to eat of it, to receive his heritage and rejoice in his labor—this is the gift of God.

—ECCLESIASTES 5:19

Lord, I pray that (husband's name) will find it easy to give to You and to others as You have instructed in Your Word. Give him wisdom to handle money wisely. Help him make good decisions as to how he spends. Show him how to plan for the future. I pray that he will find the perfect balance between spending needlessly and being miserly. May he always be paid well for the work he does, and may his money not be stolen, lost, devoured, destroyed, or wasted.

Prayer Journal

_____

_____

_____

_____

_____

_____

_____

_____

_____

_____

_____

_____

_____

_____

_____

_____

_____

_____

_____

_____

_____

_____

_____

_____

_____

_____

_____

_____

_____

Prayer Journal

...help him handle money wisely

I have been young, and now am old; yet I have not seen the righteous forsaken, nor his descendants begging bread.

—PSALM 37:25

Lord, help both of us to remember that all we have belongs to You and to be grateful for it. May we be good stewards of all that You give us, and walk in total agreement as to how it is to be dispersed. I pray that we will learn to live free of burdensome debt. Where we have not been wise, bring restoration and give us guidance. Show me how I can help increase our finances and not decrease them unwisely.

Prayer Journal

Prayer Journal

...all we have belongs to You

Drink water from your own cistern, and running water from your own well. Should your fountains be dispersed abroad, streams of water in the streets? Let them be only your own, and not for strangers with you. Let your fountain be blessed, and rejoice with the wife of your youth.

—PROVERBS 5:15-18

Lord, I realize that an important part of my ministry to my husband is sexual. Help me to never use sex as a weapon or a means of manipulation by giving and withholding it for selfish reasons. I commit this area of our lives to You, Lord. May it be continually new and alive. Make it all that You created it to be. I pray that we will desire each other and no one else. Show me how to make myself attractive and desirable to my husband and be the kind of partner he needs. I pray that neither of us will ever be tempted to think about seeking fulfillment elsewhere.

Prayer Journal

Prayer Journal

...be the kind of partner he needs

If anyone is in Christ, he is a new creation;
old things have passed away; behold, all
things have become new.

—2 CORINTHIANS 5:17-18

Lord, deliver us from the bondage of
past mistakes. Remove from our midst
the effects of any sexual experience—in
thought or deed—that happened outside
of our relationship. Take away anyone
or anything from our lives that would
inspire temptation to infidelity. Help us
to "abstain from sexual immorality" so
that each of us will know "how to pos-
sess his own vessel in sanctification and
honor" (1 Thessalonians 4:4). I pray
that we will make time for one another,
communicate our true feelings openly,
and remain sensitive to what each other
needs.

Prayer Journal

Prayer Journal

_____
_____
_____
_____
_____
_____
_____
_____
_____
_____
_____
_____
_____
_____
_____
_____
_____
_____
_____
_____
_____
_____
_____
_____
_____
_____
_____

...sanctification and honor

If there is any consolation in Christ, if any comfort of love, if any fellowship of the Spirit, if any affection and mercy, fulfill my joy by being like-minded, having the same love, being of one accord, of one mind.

—PHILIPPIANS 2:1-2

Lord, help my husband and me to demonstrate how much we care for and value each other. Remind us throughout each day to affectionately touch one another in some way. Help us to not be cold, undemonstrative, uninterested, or remote. Enable us to be warm, tender, compassionate, loving, and adoring. Break through any hardheadedness on our part that refuses to change and grow. If one of us is less affectionate to the other's detriment, bring us into balance.

Prayer Journal

...warm, tender,
compassionate, loving

His left hand is under my head, and his right hand embraces me.

—SONG OF SOLOMON 2:6

Lord, may we not so take each other for granted that we don't make the effort to reach out and touch one another with affection. Help us not to weaken our marriage through neglect of this vital means of communication. I pray that we always "greet one another with a kiss of love" (1 Peter 5:14). I know that only the transforming power of the Holy Spirit can make changes that last. I trust You to transform us and make us the husband and wife You called us to be.

Prayer Journal

Prayer Journal

_____

_____

_____

_____

_____

_____

_____

_____

_____

_____

_____

_____

_____

_____

_____

_____

_____

_____

_____

_____

_____

_____

_____

_____

_____

*...let us touch one another
with affection*

Blessed is the man who endures temptation;
for when he has been approved, he will
receive the crown of life which the Lord has
promised to those who love Him.

—JAMES 1:12

Lord, I pray that (husband's name) will
not be broken down by the power of
evil, but raised up by the power of God.
Establish a wall of protection around
him. Fill him with Your Spirit and flush
out all that is not of You. Help him to
take charge over his own spirit and have
self-control to resist anything and anyone who becomes a lure. I pray that You
would strengthen my husband to resist
any temptation that comes his way.

Prayer Journal

Prayer Journal

_____

_____

_____

_____

_____

_____

_____

_____

_____

_____

_____

_____

_____

_____

_____

_____

_____

_____

_____

_____

_____

_____

_____

_____

_____

_____

_____

_____

_____

...fill him with Your Spirit

Examine me, O LORD, and prove me; try my mind and my heart. For Your lovingkindness is before my eyes, and I have walked in Your truth.

—PSALM 26:2-3

Lord, shield my husband's mind from the lies of the enemy. Help him to clearly discern between Your voice and any other, and show him how to take every thought captive as You have instructed us to do. May he thirst for Your Word and hunger for Your truth so that he can recognize wrong thinking. Remind him again today that he has the mind of Christ.

Prayer Journal

Prayer Journal

_____
_____
_____
_____
_____
_____
_____
_____
_____
_____
_____
_____
_____
_____
_____
_____
_____
_____
_____
_____
_____
_____
_____
_____
_____
_____
_____
_____
_____
_____

...he has the mind of Christ

You will keep him in perfect peace, whose
mind is stayed on You, because he trusts in
You.

—ISAIAH 26:3

Lord, help (husband's name) to be anxious
for nothing, but in everything by prayer
and supplication, with thanksgiving, let
his requests be made known to You; and
may Your peace, which surpasses all
understanding, guard his heart and mind
through Christ Jesus (Philippians 4:6-7).
And whatever things are true, noble, just,
pure, lovely, of good report, having virtue,
or anything praiseworthy, let him think on
these things (Philippians 4:8).

Prayer Journal

Prayer Journal

...guard his heart and mind

The LORD is my light and my salvation;
whom shall I fear? The LORD is the strength
of my life; of whom shall I be afraid?

—PSALM 27:1

Lord, I pray You will perfect (husband's name) in Your love so that fear finds no place in him. I know You have not given him a spirit of fear. You've given him power, love, and a sound mind (2 Timothy 1:7). I pray in the name of Jesus that fear will not rule over (husband's name). Instead, may Your Word penetrate every fiber of his being, convincing him that Your love for him is far greater than anything he faces and nothing can separate him from it.

Prayer Journal

Prayer Journal

...power, love, and a sound mind

Behold, the eye of the LORD is on those who
fear Him, on those who hope in His mercy.

—PSALM 33:18

Lord, deliver (husband's name) this day
from fear that destroys and replace it
with godly fear (Jeremiah 32:40). Teach
him Your way, O Lord. Help him to
walk in Your truth. Unite his heart to
fear Your name (Psalm 86:11). May he
have no fear of men, but rise up and
boldly say, "The LORD is my helper; I
will not fear. What can man do to me?"
(Hebrews 13:6) and, "How great is
Your goodness, which You have laid up
for those who fear You, which You have
prepared for those who trust in You"
(Psalm 31:19).

Prayer Journal

Prayer Journal

...how great is Your goodness

As God has distributed to each one, as the
Lord has called each one, so let him walk.

—1 Corinthians 7:17

Lord, when You call us, You also enable
us. Enable my husband to walk worthy
of his calling and become the man of
God You made him to be. Continue to
remind him of what You've called him
to, and don't let him get sidetracked
with things that are unessential to Your
plan for his life. Lift his eyes above the
circumstances of the moment so he can
see the purpose for which You created
him.

Prayer Journal

The Power of a Praying Wife

Prayer Journal

...You call us for Your purposes

Lord, help (husband's name) to realize who he is in Christ and give him certainty that he was created for a high purpose. May the eyes of his understanding be enlightened so that he will know what is the hope of Your calling (Ephesians 1:18). I pray that the desires of his heart will not be in conflict with the desires of Yours. May he seek You for direction, and hear when You speak to his soul.

Prayer Journal

Prayer Journal

_____
_____
_____
_____
_____
_____
_____
_____
_____
_____
_____
_____
_____
_____
_____
_____
_____
_____
_____
_____
_____
_____
_____
_____
_____
_____
_____

...created for a high purpose

But as for me, I would seek God, and to God
I would commit my cause.

—JOB 5:8

Lord, give (husband's name) daily discernment to make decisions based on Your revelation. Help him to make godly choices and keep him from doing anything foolish. Take foolishness out of his heart and enable him to quickly recognize error and avoid it. Open his eyes to clearly see the consequences of any anticipated behavior. May he reverence You and Your ways and seek to know Your truth.

Prayer Journal

Prayer Journal

...make godly choices

If any of you lacks wisdom, let him ask of
God, who gives to all liberally and without
reproach, and it will be given to him.

—JAMES 1:5-6

Lord, please instruct my husband even as
he is sleeping (Psalm 16:7), and in the
morning, I pray he will do what's right
rather than follow the leading of his own
flesh. I know the wisdom of this world is
foolishness with You, Lord (1 Corinthians
3:19). May he not buy into it, but keep
his eyes on You and have ears to hear
Your voice.

Prayer Journal

Prayer Journal

...give him ears to hear Your voice

Bless the LORD, *O my soul, and forget not all*
His benefits: who forgives all your iniquities,
who heals all your diseases.

—PSALM 103:2-3

Lord, when my husband is ill, I pray
You will sustain him and heal him. Fill
him with Your joy to give him strength.
Specifically, I pray for (mention any area
of concern). Give him faith to say, "'O
LORD my God, I cried out to You, and
You healed me' [Psalm 30:2]. Thank
You, Lord, that You are my healer." I
pray that my husband will live a long
and healthy life.

Prayer Journal

The Power of a Praying Wife

...fill him with Your joy

Beloved, I pray that you may prosper in all things and be in health, just as your soul prospers.

—3 JOHN 2

Lord, I pray that (husband's name) will have the desire to take care of his body, to eat the kind of food that brings health, to get regular exercise, and avoid anything that would be harmful to him. Help him to understand that his body is Your temple, and he should care for it as such (1 Corinthians 3:16). I pray that he will present it as a living sacrifice, holy and acceptable to You (Romans 12:1).

Prayer Journal

Prayer Journal

_____
_____
_____
_____
_____
_____
_____
_____
_____
_____
_____
_____
_____
_____
_____
_____
_____
_____
_____
_____
_____
_____
_____
_____
_____
_____
_____
_____

...holy and acceptable to You

The Lord is my rock and my fortress and my deliverer; my God, my strength, in whom I will trust; my shield and the horn of my salvation, my stronghold. I will call upon the Lord, who is worthy to be praised; so shall I be saved from my enemies.

—PSALM 18:2-3

Lord, watch over my husband, and keep him safe, especially in cars and planes. Hide him from violence and the plans of evil people. Wherever he walks, secure his steps. Keep him on Your path so that his feet don't slip (Psalm 17:5). If his foot does slip, hold him up by Your mercy (Psalm 94:18). Give him the wisdom and discretion that will help him walk safely and not fall into danger (Proverbs 3:21-23).

Prayer Journal

The Power of a Praying Wife

Prayer Journal

...hold him up by Your mercy

In the time of trouble He shall hide me in His pavilion; in the secret place of His tabernacle He shall hide me; He shall set me high upon a rock.

—PSALM 27:5

Lord, I pray today that You would be my husband's fortress, strength, shield, and stronghold (Psalm 18:2-3). Make him to dwell in the shadow of Your wings (Psalm 91:1-2). Be his rock, salvation, and defense, so that he will not be moved or shaken (Psalm 62:6). I pray that even though bad things may be happening all around him, they will not come near him (Psalm 91:7).

Prayer Journal

Prayer Journal

...the shadow of Your wings

Cast your burden on the LORD, and He shall sustain you; He shall never permit the righteous to be moved.

—PSALM 55:22

Lord, I know You work great things in the midst of trials. Help me support (husband's name) with prayer and encouragement so that he will get through every battle as a winner. You are our refuge and strength, a very present help in trouble (Psalm 46:1). Build up my husband so that no matter what happens he will be able to stand strong through it.

Prayer Journal

Prayer Journal

_____
_____
_____
_____
_____
_____
_____
_____
_____
_____
_____
_____
_____
_____
_____
_____
_____
_____
_____
_____
_____
_____
_____
_____
_____
_____
_____

...our refuge and strength

Through the LORD's mercies we are not consumed, because His compassions fail not. They are new every morning; great is Your faithfulness.

—LAMENTATIONS 3:22-23

Lord, You have invited us to "come boldly to the throne of grace, that we may obtain mercy and find grace to help in time of need" (Hebrews 4:16). I come before Your throne and ask for grace for my husband. Strengthen his heart for this battle and give him patience to wait on You (Psalm 27:1-4). Help him to be always "rejoicing in hope, patient in tribulation, continuing steadfastly in prayer" (Romans 12:12).

Prayer Journal

Prayer Journal

_____
_____
_____
_____
_____
_____
_____
_____
_____
_____
_____
_____
_____
_____
_____
_____
_____
_____
_____
_____
_____
_____
_____
_____
_____
_____
_____
_____

...obtain mercy and find grace

*Let integrity and uprightness preserve me, for
I wait for You.*

—PSALM 25:21

Lord, I pray You would help (husband's
name) to be a man of great integrity.
Guide him by Your Spirit of truth at all
times (John 16:13). Be with him to bear
witness to the truth so that in times of
pressure he will act on it with confidence. Bind mercy and truth around his
neck and write them on the tablet of his
heart so he will find favor and high
esteem in the sight of God and man
(Proverbs 3:3-4).

Prayer Journal

Prayer Journal

_____

_____

_____

_____

_____

_____

_____

_____

_____

_____

_____

_____

_____

_____

_____

_____

_____

_____

_____

_____

_____

_____

_____

_____

_____

_____

_____

_____

...favor and high esteem

Vindicate me, O LORD, *for I have walked in my integrity. I have also trusted in the* LORD; *I shall not slip.*

—PSALM 26:1

Lord, give my husband the strength to say "yes" when he should say "yes," and courage to say "no" when he should say "no." Enable him to stand for what he knows is right and not waver under pressure from the world. Give him a teachable spirit that is willing to listen to the voice of wisdom and grow in Your ways.

Prayer Journal

Prayer Journal

_____

_____

_____

_____

_____

_____

_____

_____

_____

_____

_____

_____

_____

_____

_____

_____

_____

_____

_____

_____

_____

_____

_____

_____

_____

...grow in Your ways

By humility and the fear of the LORD are riches and honor and life.

—PROVERBS 22:4

Lord, I pray over my husband's reputation. I ask that (husband's name) will bear good fruit out of the goodness that is within him, and that he will be known by the good that he does. May the fruits of honesty, trustworthiness, and humility sweeten all his dealings so that his reputation will never be spoiled.

Prayer Journal

Prayer Journal

_...be known by the good
that he does_

Who shall bring a charge against God's elect?
It is God who justifies. Who is he who con-
demns? It is Christ who died, and furthermore
is also risen, who is even at the right hand of
God, who also makes intercession for us.

—ROMANS 8:33-34

Lord, may (husband's name) trust in You and not be afraid of what man can do to him (Psalm 56:11). For You have said whoever believes in You will not be put to shame (Romans 10:11). Lead him, guide him, and be his mighty fortress and hiding place. May his light so shine before men that they see his good works and glorify You, Lord (Matthew 5:16).

Prayer Journal

Prayer Journal

...may his light shine

A faithful man will abound with blessings.

—PROVERBS 28:20

Lord, speak to (husband's name) about making Your Word, prayer, and praise a priority. Enable him to place our children and me in greater prominence in his heart than career, friends, and activities. I pray he will seek You first and submit his all to You, for when he does I know the other pieces of his life will fit together perfectly.

Prayer Journal

Prayer Journal

...seek You first

*Let us consider one another in order to stir up
love and good works, not forsaking the
assembling of ourselves together, as is the
manner of some, but exhorting one another.*

—HEBREWS 10:24-25

Lord, show (husband's name) what it
means to be a true friend and enable
him to be one. I pray my husband would
have good, godly male friends with
whom he can openly share his heart.
May they be trustworthy men of wisdom who will speak truth into his life
and not just say what he wants to hear.
Show him the importance of godly
friendships and help me encourage him
to sustain them.

Prayer Journal

The Power of a Praying Wife

Prayer Journal

...a true friend

A friend loves at all times, and a brother is born for adversity.

—PROVERBS 17:17

Lord, I pray for strong, peaceful relationships with each of my husband's family members, neighbors, acquaintances, and coworkers. Inspire open communication and mutual acceptance between them. Let there be reconciliation where there has been estrangement. Work peace into anything that needs to be worked out. Enable (husband's name) to be a forgiving person and not carry grudges or hold things in his heart against others.

Prayer Journal

Prayer Journal

_____
_____
_____
_____
_____
_____
_____
_____
_____
_____
_____
_____
_____
_____
_____
_____
_____
_____
_____
_____
_____
_____
_____
_____
_____
_____
_____
_____

...strong, peaceful relationships

I will be a Father to you, and you shall be My
sons and daughters, says the LORD *Almighty.*

—2 CORINTHIANS 6:18

Lord, give (husband's name) fresh revelation of You today and a hunger in his
heart to really know You as his heavenly
Father. Draw him close to spend time in
Your presence so he can become more
like You and fully understand Your
Father's heart of compassion and love
toward him. Grow that same heart in
him for his children. Help him to balance mercy, judgment, and instruction
the way You do.

Prayer Journal

Prayer Journal

_____
_____
_____
_____
_____
_____
_____
_____
_____
_____
_____
_____
_____
_____
_____
_____
_____
_____
_____
_____
_____
_____
_____
_____
_____
_____
_____

...draw him close

*Listen to me, my children; pay attention to
the words of my mouth.*

—PROVERBS 7:24

Lord, give (husband's name) skills of
communication with his children. Help
him to be kind, loving, soft-hearted,
warm, interested, affirming, affectionate,
involved, strong, consistent, dependable,
verbally communicative, understanding,
and patient. May he require and inspire
his children to honor him as their father
so that their lives will be long and
blessed. Being a good father is some-
thing (husband's name) wants very
much. I pray that You would give him
the desire of his heart.

Prayer Journal

Prayer Journal

...help him inspire his children

Put off, concerning your former conduct, the old man which grows corrupt according to the deceitful lusts, and be renewed in the spirit of your mind, and . . . put on the new man which was created according to God, in true righteousness and holiness.

—EPHESIANS 4:22-24

Lord, wherever my husband's past has become an unpleasant memory, I pray You would redeem it and bring life out of it. Bind up his wounds (Psalm 147:3). Restore his soul (Psalm 23:3). Help him to release the past so that he will not live in it, but learn from it, break out of it, and move into the future You have for him.

Prayer Journal

_____
_____
_____
_____
_____
_____
_____
_____
_____
_____
_____
_____
_____
_____
_____
_____
_____
_____
_____
_____
_____
_____
_____
_____
_____
_____
_____
_____

Prayer Journal

_____
_____
_____
_____
_____
_____
_____
_____
_____
_____
_____
_____
_____
_____
_____
_____
_____
_____
_____
_____
_____
_____
_____
_____
_____
_____

...release the past

Therefore, as the elect of God, holy and beloved, put on tender mercies, kindness, humility, meekness, longsuffering; bearing with one another, and forgiving one another.

—COLOSSIANS 3:12-13

Lord, I pray that (husband's name) will be kind and patient, not selfish or easily provoked. Enable him to bear all things, believe all things, hope all things, and endure all things (1 Corinthians 13:7). Release him from anger, unrest, anxiety, concerns, inner turmoil, strife, and pressure. May he not be broken in spirit because of sorrow (Proverbs 15:13), but enjoy the continual feast of a merry heart (Proverbs 15:15).

Prayer Journal

Prayer Journal

...enjoy a merry heart

The LORD will give strength to His people;
the LORD will bless His people with peace.

—PSALM 29:11

Lord, help my husband to be anxious for nothing, but give thanks in all things so he can know the peace that passes all understanding. May he come to the point of saying, "I have learned in whatever state I am, to be content" (Philippians 4:11). Please fill him with Your love and peace today. May there be a calmness, serenity, and sense of well-being established in him because his life is God-controlled, rather than flesh-controlled.

Prayer Journal

Prayer Journal

...be anxious for nothing

I am my beloved's, and my beloved is mine.

—SONG OF SOLOMON 6:3

Lord, please bless our marriage. Shield it from our own selfishness and neglect, from the evil plans and desires of others, and from unhealthy or dangerous situations. May there be no thoughts of divorce or infidelity in our hearts, and none in our future. Set us free from past hurts, memories, and ties from previous relationships, and unrealistic expectations of one another.

Prayer Journal

The Power of a Praying Wife

Prayer Journal

_____

_____

_____

_____

_____

_____

_____

_____

_____

_____

_____

_____

_____

_____

_____

_____

_____

_____

_____

_____

_____

_____

_____

_____

_____

_____

_____

_____

_____

...bless our marriage

*Therefore a man shall leave his father and
mother and be joined to his wife, and they
shall become one flesh.*

—GENESIS 2:24

Lord, help us to make time for one
another alone, to nurture and renew the
marriage and remind ourselves of the
reasons we were married in the first
place. I pray that (husband's name) will
be so committed to You that his com-
mitment to me will not waver, no matter
what storms come. I pray that our love
for each other will grow stronger every
day, so that we will never leave a legacy
of divorce to our children.

Prayer Journal

Prayer Journal

...grow stronger every day

The LORD redeems the soul of His servants,
and none of those who trust in Him shall be
condemned.

—PSALM 34:22

Lord, I pray that (husband's name) would have faith in You to redeem his soul from negative emotions. Specifically I pray about (area of concern). Deliver him from this and all other controlling emotions. I know that only You can deliver and heal, but use me as Your instrument of restoration. Enable me to understand and have words to say that will bring comfort and life.

Prayer Journal

Prayer Journal

...redeem his soul

Then our mouth was filled with laughter, and our tongue with singing....The LORD has done great things for us, and we are glad.

—PSALM 126:2-3

Lord, please free (husband's name) to share his deepest feelings with me and others who can help. Liberate him to cry when he needs to and not bottle his emotions inside. At the same time, give him the gift of laughter and ability to find humor in even serious situations. Teach him to take his eyes off his circumstances and trust in You, regardless of how he is feeling.

Prayer Journal

Prayer Journal

_____
_____
_____
_____
_____
_____
_____
_____
_____
_____
_____
_____
_____
_____
_____
_____
_____
_____
_____
_____
_____
_____
_____
_____
_____
_____
_____
_____
_____

...the gift of laughter

He who walks righteously and speaks uprightly...he will dwell on high; his place of defense will be the fortress of rocks; bread will be given him, his water will be sure.

—ISAIAH 33:15-16

Lord, lead (husband's name) today in *Your* light, teach him *Your* way, so he will walk in *Your* truth. I pray that he would have a deeper walk with You and an ever-progressing hunger for Your Word. May Your presence be like a delicacy he never ceases to crave. Lead him on Your path and make him quick to confess when he strays from it. Reveal to him any hidden sin that would hinder him from walking rightly before You.

Prayer Journal

Prayer Journal

...a deeper walk with You

Walk worthy of the calling with which you were called, with all lowliness and gentleness, with long-suffering, bearing with one another in love.

—EPHESIANS 4:1-2

Lord, I pray that You will enable (husband's name) to walk in the Spirit and not in the flesh and thereby keep himself "from the paths of the destroyer" (Psalm 17:4). As he walks in the Spirit, may he bear the fruit of the Spirit, which is love, joy, peace, patience, kindness, goodness, faithfulness, gentleness, and self-control (Galatians 5:22-23). Keep him on the Highway of Holiness so that the way he walks will be integrated into every part of his life.

Prayer Journal

Prayer Journal

...bear the fruit of the Spirit

Whoever guards his mouth and tongue keeps
his soul from troubles.

—PROVERBS 21:23

Lord, help us to show each other
respect, speak words that encourage,
share our feelings openly, and come to
mutual agreements without strife.
You've said in Your Word that when
two agree, You are in their midst. I pray
that the reverse be true as well—that
You will be in our midst so that we two
can agree. Let the words of our mouths
and the meditations of our hearts be
acceptable in Your sight, O Lord, our
strength and our Redeemer (Psalm
19:14).

Prayer Journal

...speak words that encourage

He who covers his sins will not prosper, but whoever confesses and forsakes them will have mercy.

—PROVERBS 28:13

Lord, I pray You would cleanse (husband's name) from any secret sins and teach him to be a person who is quick to confess when he is wrong (Psalm 19:12). Bring him to full repentance before You. I know that humility must come before honor (Proverbs 15:33). Take away all pride that would cause him to deny his faults and work into his soul a humility of heart so that he will receive the honor You have for him.

Prayer Journal

Prayer Journal

_____

_____

_____

_____

_____

_____

_____

_____

_____

_____

_____

_____

_____

_____

_____

_____

_____

_____

_____

_____

_____

_____

_____

_____

_____

_____

_____

_____

...humility of heart

You have delivered my soul from death. Have You not delivered my feet from falling, that I may walk before God in the light of the living?

—PSALM 56:13

Lord, I call upon You and ask that You would work deliverance in my husband's life. Deliver him from anything that binds him. Set him free from (name a specific thing). Deliver him quickly and be a rock of refuge and a fortress of defense to save him (Psalm 31:2). If the deliverance he prays for isn't immediate, keep him from discouragement and help him to be confident that You have begun a good work in him and will complete it (Philippians 1:6).

Prayer Journal

Prayer Journal

_____
_____
_____
_____
_____
_____
_____
_____
_____
_____
_____
_____
_____
_____
_____
_____
_____
_____
_____
_____
_____
_____
_____
_____
_____
_____
_____
_____
_____

...rock of refuge, fortress of defense

The LORD shall help them and deliver them;
He shall deliver them from the wicked, and
save them, because they trust in Him.

—PSALM 37:40

Lord, I pray today that (husband's name) will be strong in You and put on the whole armor of God, so he can stand against the wiles of the devil in the evil day. Give him the certainty that even in his most hopeless state, when he finds it impossible to change anything, You, Lord, can change everything. You have said to call upon You in the day of trouble and You will deliver us (Psalm 50:15).

Prayer Journal

Prayer Journal

...*You, Lord,*
can change everything

Though He was a Son, yet He learned obedience by the things which He suffered. And having been perfected, He became the author of eternal salvation to all who obey Him.

—Hebrews 5:8-9

Lord, I pray that You would give (husband's name) a desire to live in obedience to Your laws and Your ways. Reward him according to his righteousness and according to the cleanness of his hands (Psalm 18:20). Help him to hear Your specific instructions to him and enable him to obey them. Give him a heart that longs to do Your will, and may he enjoy the peace that can only come from living in total obedience to Your commands.

Prayer Journal

Prayer Journal

...enable him to obey

*You have put off the old man with his deeds,
and have put on the new man who is renewed
in knowledge according to the image of Him
who created him.*

—COLOSSIANS 3:9-10

Lord, may (husband's name) recognize the
unique qualities You've placed in him and
be able to appreciate them. Give him the
peace and security of knowing that he is
accepted, not rejected, by You. Free him
from the self-focus and self-consciousness
that can imprison his soul. Help him to
see who *You* really are so he'll know who
he really is. May his true self-image be the
image of Christ stamped upon his soul.

Prayer Journal

Prayer Journal

...help him to know who he is

For I am not ashamed of the gospel of Christ,
for it is the power of God to salvation for
everyone who believes, for the Jew first and
also for the Greek. For in it the righteousness
of God is revealed from faith to faith; as it is
written, "The just shall live by faith."

—ROMANS 1:16-17

Lord, feed my husband's soul with
Your Word so his faith grows big
enough to believe that with You all
things are possible (Matthew 19:26).
Give him unfailing certainty that what
You've promised to do, You will do
(Romans 4:21). Make his faith a shield
of protection for him. Put it into action
to move the mountains in his life. Your
Word says, "The just shall live by
faith" (Romans 1:17); I pray that he
will live the kind of faith-filled life
You've called us all to experience.

Prayer Journal

Prayer Journal

...the just shall live by faith

Mark the blameless man, and observe the
upright; for the future of that man is peace.

—PSALM 37:37

Lord, may (husband's name) live with leading from the Holy Spirit and not walk in doubt and fear of what may happen in the days that lie ahead. Help him to mature and grow in You daily, submitting to You all his dreams and desires, knowing that "the things which are impossible with men are possible with God" (Luke 18:27). Give him God-ordained goals, and show him how to conduct himself in a way that always invests in his future.

Prayer Journal

Prayer Journal

...all his dreams and desires

There is hope in your future, says the LORD.

—JEREMIAH 31:17

Lord, I pray that You would plant my husband firmly in Your house and keep him fresh and flourishing and bearing fruit into old age (Psalm 92:13-14). And when it comes time for him to leave this earth and go to be with You, may he have such a strong vision for his eternal future that it makes his transition smooth, painless, and accompanied by peace and joy. Until that day, I pray he will find the vision for his future in You.

Prayer Journal

The Power of a Praying Wife

Prayer Journal

...his eternal future